A
Woman's Book
of
Grieving

A
Woman's Book
of
Grieving

Nessa
Rapoport

· · · · · ·

Linocuts:
Rochelle Rubinstein Kaplan

· · · · · ·

William Morrow and Company, Inc.
New York

It is the policy of William Morrow and Company, Inc.,
and its imprints and affiliates, recognizing the importance of
preserving what has been written, to print the books we publish
on acid-free paper, and we exert our best efforts to that end.

Library of Congress Cataloging-in-Publication Data

Rapoport, Nessa.
A woman's book of grieving / Nessa Rapoport :
linocuts, Rochelle Rubinstein Kaplan.
p.   cm.
ISBN 0688-10947-0
1. Grief. 2. Loss (Psychology). 3. Bereavement—Psychological
aspects. 4. Death—Psychological aspects. 5. Women—Psychology. 6. Meditations.   1. Title.
BF575.G7R358   1994
811'.54—dc20   93-23201
CIP
Printed in the United States of America

2   3   4   5   6   7   8   9   10
BOOK DESIGN BY KRYSTYNA SKALSKI

To honor the memory of

JORDAN FLEISCHNER METZGER

and

AILIE MUIRHEAD GRUSEKE

Contents

FRIEND OF MY YOUTH

HERE IS SORROW

THE RUINED SONG

SANCTUARY

TRUE WORDS

HARVEST

AN OLD TALE · 107

Friend of My Youth

SUE—AND OURSELVES

Flying between two cities, I sit beside a woman who, like me, is reading her manuscript. Neither of us means to speak, and yet we do, sanctioned by coincidence. What are you writing of? she asks. Grief, I answer her. She says, My best friend in the world just died. The accident in England: Did you hear? The ferry tipped, I prayed she wasn't on it, but she was, I still cannot believe that she's not here. I speak then of Lynda, someone I loved for almost twenty years. Of all my friends, I say, Lynda had by far the most vitality. That was my friend's name, Sue tells me quietly. We stare at each other without words.

This book is for Sue, and for all of us compelled to face the next frontier: news that seems too difficult to bear.

FRIEND OF MY YOUTH

Friend of my youth, three years ago I stepped down from the bus and you were there, your face a little older from the battle, with someone else's hair. It was spring where you lived, and your three girls had much to say to me, visitor for an afternoon on your farm, far from the city, farther from the place where you were born. Slowly the beautiful day's light turned dark. The windows were open as you gave me supper; the last bus would soon depart. I hugged you hard. Your husband drove me into town in silence. "Whatever happens," he finally said, "nothing will ever be the same."

LYNDA

Four years later, your husband has remarried, and your little girls turn into women without you, and your sister tells me how your mother's sick with what had stricken you, and how one evening when your youngest girl was ill, and she, your mother, sat beside her, ready to console, the girl ran to the new wife you would have wished for him, whimpering, "My head hurts," and lay down upon her lap, and how your mother rejoiced: The love she bears in her relinquishing is as large as you would have wanted for your daughters. Lynda, I remember precisely who you were, and when they're grown I'll try to tell them everything.

Here Is Sorrow

UNDO IT, TAKE IT BACK

Undo it, take it back, make every day the previous one
until I am returned to the day before the one that made
you gone. Or set me on an airplane traveling west,
crossing the date line again and again, losing this day,
then that, until the day of loss still lies ahead, and you
are here instead of sorrow.

NO ONE AHEAD OF ME

No one ahead of me on the front line, standing before the fire, willing to be consumed to give me life. No larger shadow daunting me, no one to emulate or to disdain, no body that birthed me growing older in my sight. Now I can look; there's nothing to deflect or mask my vision. On the far side of the chasm is the place where you have gone. For the first time, you will not reach out to save me.

ARMS THAT BAKED A THOUSAND CAKES

Someone has stripped the top layer of my skin. Now anyone in pain knows me. The child whose mother says, "If you don't stop, I'm leaving you behind," is crying in the supermarket, and I, grown, am crying: "Rock me, missing mother. Arms that baked a thousand cakes, cradle me, dissolve me in your house of earth, while I dissolve under fluorescent light, weeping for the comfort of your dark earth arms." And you, as if we were still walking in a wood, thrust at the underbrush to clear a way for me, your daughter, unable to follow you.

CRY

Flesh of my flesh, bone of my bone, sister. Blood of my blood, born of my earliest thought. Cry of my cry, how do we find ourselves sitting on these low chairs? Where is the one who greeted us with still-wet hands? The dishes are put away, the day is done. And all the laughter in this house is gone.

THE BODY IN GRIEF

The body in grief is not a pretty thing. The lined skin and worried eyes, the fretful hands without repose, the frame bent or swollen, like an armchair sat on one too many times: I am the woman who once stood in the dark, waiting for you to begin, fragrant with lily and jasmine, not afraid. Now pleasure tastes like ash; your nakedness is in the grave.

ALL DAY I DREAM OF SLEEP

All day I dream of sleep, its lakes of sheets, pillows in undulating heaps. I want to mate my body to my bed, float in languor, infused, etherous. But when at last the night makes its descent, my body is a stranger, resisting all blandishment, and your face, your face, the only living thing.

DROWNING IN REMEMBRANCE

Drowning in remembrance, looming faces and taunting mouths, the language of love mocking, looking up at the mottled weedy surface, the sun a weak disc, the days a tide current pulling me down into a light that eats itself, away from an outstretched arm or any solace, I surrender, you have left me, and I hate you for it.

AT THE END OF THIS GAME

At the end of this game, the mighty have fallen and only two pawns remain. The light against the dark: Which will prevail? When charity is veiled and love outlawed, the choice is stark. Choose light, the ancient voices plead with me. Rail against what seems to be ordained. But I choose dark. And with exquisite pleasure, I give up.

FROM THE DARKEST PLACE

From the darkest place, base of the shattered stairs, the
stony voice says: Never, and: No, and: Unforgiven, but
I, volleying against despair, still cry out in the habit of
hopefulness: Find me, lift me up, bathe me in forgotten
grace.

The Ruined Song

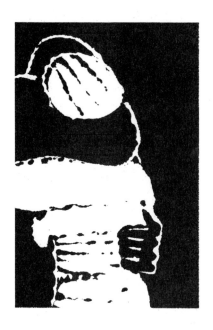

RESURRECTION

Here, you said
handed me
thin book of a
dead woman

Fifty years ago
she stood in snow
waiting for one word:
Alive. Murdered.
Can you tell this?
the women whispered
how we stood in gray light
silent until night

In a dark room
a doctor bends
over shadowy film
and in a gray room
imprisoned by fear
(can you tell this?)
I wait for one word

Shield me from sorrow
her son in his cell
her book in my hand
a mother's breast
X ray of grief and tenderness
saving

AMAZON

The woman with too-short hair
is visiting the house
of the daughter whose mother ails
with too-short hair

A seam where once
softness stood
a side of sacrifice
a side of solitude

To save the whole
they cut away the part
lying in the dark
a woman crying

Beneath closed eyes
a beaded wedding dress
the rise and fall of breath
shy husband's hands

The reaper who hates women
has taken away her hair
her head is bare
no one can comfort her

Another woman's hair
sits on her head
one side softness
one side dead

The reaper who hates women
bequeaths a spiteful gift
of mother against daughter
nourishing the dark

In the house of women
with too-short hair
no one is spared
no one is spared

MOURNING SONG

Was, was not
There, not there
Her empty chair

Her chair
No body there
Air

Where?
All gone
Wrong

Wronged
Why?
Ayyy

Lamentations

HOWL

I am the lost baby, howling in night, annihilated by longing I cannot moderate or excise, needing you without being able to speak, before words, their tempering lies, tales of meeting in another life or hackneyed reassurances: Life will go on. It will, I know, go on and on and on, relentless, no reprieve from consciousness.

RAGE

What can contain this rage? What pot, suitcase, tanker, silo, planet can hold without explosion such a magnitude? Harness me, disarm my bellowing, ship me out of my vibrating solitude, condemned to such a murderous rage, dying of anger, sacrificed.

I WANT

I want this one's hair and that one's father; this one's face and that one's lover; this one's house and that one's toy; this one's youth and that one's child. Before, I envied no living thing. Now everyone has something that I covet.

TELL EVERYONE

Wail, scream, shriek, flail limbs. Be primitive for once, hold nothing back. Beat fists upon the earth. Tell everyone. Throw aside decorum and restraint, strip reserve, junk propriety. Unveil yourself of every falsity, all that you withheld for future's sake, all ideas of next year or next week. Dispose of dreams, jeer at signs of life. Tell everyone.

THE ANTICIPATION OF SORROW

The anticipation of sorrow is sick-making, a hand clutched to the chest, the stalling of all hope against the heart. It is rib-binding, imprisoning the breath. If for a moment you forget, and the day becomes like any previous one, and you step outside, briefly unencumbered, and the earth seems radiant as you walk, then with the wing-rush of a carrion bird the news descends, and it is doubly grim: The sky is blotted out, the light besmirched, and the weary world crawls forward, ancient but determined to arrive at its non-negotiable destination.

Night Thoughts

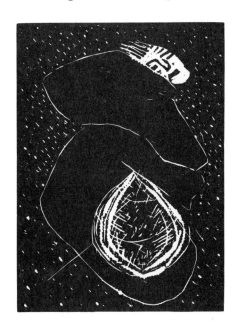

SUFFERING

When grief descends, there is no redemption then in suffering, nothing saving or luminous about it, no higher meaning to its torment, not one gleaning of wisdom or grace. Every moment's pain, like a parody of first love, afflicts for hours, and every day flaunts its eternity. If we could choose our lot, who would not say: Woman, when you see suffering, run, flee from it. But we cannot choose.

In those days a woman would give all she has to get just one thing back. No one wants to learn from pain. When first the ship founders, who thinks of booty? In a catastrophe, who conceives of profit? No, she bewails her fate. Night after night, she reviews her case: Had I even the faintest augury? She compares in stealth her own plight to her neighbors': Surely I've lost the most; all others seem unscathed.

When you meet such a woman, do not speak of inner sustenance, of benefit from sorrow or of healing. Nothing but restoration would suffice, and every day the anguish, rather than abating, multiplies. Do not say that time repairs, or talk of moving forward or of growing. Such consolations are absurd. Offer only this: I, too, have suffered and endured.

A woman who has suffered sees that all the striving in the world, all the material fruits of ardent labor, cannot buy a day's forgetting or one night's peace. She has thrust her fingers into tiny crevices of hope and clutched at the indifferent wall, but when she is compelled to let it go: what a shaming relief to stop trying. In the end, the fiercest love cannot avert the hour of dying.

As slowly as the slowest progression, the infinitesimal turning of the earth, time transports her from that day to this, with many detours, several flagrantly unfair. A month and then a year and then two pass, and it is possible to look back, admit: None of what I've understood replaces what is gone, and yet I have been forced, against my will, to learn. As vehemently as ever I protest the instrument of its acquisition, but I'll not reject a knowledge so hard-won. Now I can begin to use it and forgive the woman I was, pay tribute to her innocence.

This is the teaching of suffering, if you allow it, as if in a great stroke the world you occupy divides itself: Here is what matters; the rest—no.

Like a dancer who offers years of bloodied feet and tender injury toward a gift, a moment of perfect, elusive grace, we proceed through our buffeted lives, trying to make of ill fortune and random blows one small and beautiful thing, which all of us deserve not because of talent or means but simply because we live.

It is the hardest of all learning that the opposite of depression is not happiness—a radiant, receding goal—but vitality, to feel alive each minute you are given. Then when sweetness comes it is most sweet, and when sorrow comes you know its name. In the aftermath of suffering, you chart each day as an explorer preceding map or compass, and what you find is shockingly alloyed: All happiness is dappled, and even bleakest tragedy has moments of strange praise.

GOD CRADLED AND RETREATING

I have been to God:

a scorned lover, forsaken, like a Victorian heroine ruined by a cad, a broken engagement all she has to show for her unblemished trust;

an ungrateful daughter, bequeathed an irreplaceable gift, who takes her inheritance for granted until she has squandered it;

a bitter old woman, cheated of her savings—the confidence in good's prevailing, in love hallowed—left clutching the key to an empty box;

a despairing cynic, longing for transformation, unable to keep faith;

a convert, buoyed by the directed passion that believers know;

a baby, awed that the world can in an instant be made new, when simply to see one thing true is to taste paradise;

a bestower of blessings in return, thankful for unimagined gifts—love no longer taken for granted, fruitful work, the beauty of the created world.

God has been to me:

a lover;
a betrayer;
a magician;

a redeemer;
a confidence man;
an ample mother;
a healer;
a smiter;
a random punch;
a scathing judge;
a cold power;
a tender light.

In the middle of my days, rent by unsoothed sorrows and remorse, let me reimagine God, translated from the old man of my childhood into a great maternal love, to accommodate somehow the paradox: that every day such horrors transpire we should all take our lives, and yet the giving and receiving of love is so high a consolation we go on.

The questions the ancients asked still obtain: Why do some reap rich reward and others die barren? How can a creator allow the creatures to suffer so? How can believers murder the image of God in the body of another? How can a world rife with desecration be made whole?

SOLILOQUY

I never held her hand. I never called the last week of
her life. I meant to make the trip and then postponed
it. I said some words I never can take back.

    If only I had known.
      (Ah, but you didn't.)
    If only I had thought.
      (But you could not.)
    Why didn't I once tell you?
      (But I knew it.)
    Why didn't I invite you?
      (Never mind.)
    I hated you for growing weak, for dying.
      (I absolve you.)
    I lie awake remembering how I failed you.
      (How I love you.)
    For the rest of my life, I never—
      (Only love.)
    How could I—?
      (Don't you know you are forgiven?)
    If only—
      (Would you want your child to live with such
      reproaches?)
    No, I say reluctantly, I would not.
      (Then forgive yourself. If only I could ask you,
      that is what I'd ask.)

Normal Angel

WOMAN FRIEND

Now, when the sea and sky die quietly, deepen to black before my eye, now when my thoughts are stilled and I can dream, remembering your strong arms, the words you floated to me, the flaring light they made while I was sinking, now until true night descends, and I descend into my bed and terror of the sleep that will not come, now, until that time I am alone and, robed in you, my dress of stars, am not afraid.

LETTER TO A FRIEND WHO DID NOT
ABANDON ME

From the depths, too mute to cry, I stared at the bright world from which I'd fallen, orb narrowed to a dim slit, nearly dusk, the walls of the pit too roughly hewn to climb, clods of earth randomly assaulting, blows that seemed deserved, old words, relentless voices met with echoing applause; from that place, in which time clung airlessly, and a single second yawned into eternity; in that place where even the purity of silence was not granted me, solitude turned sour, and dreams flaunted themselves, skewed, awry; toward that place where no one dared to visit lest they, too, succumb, you stretched out your hand and would not be refused, spoke in natural tones, mused, listened without fear to frightful things, persistently cited the passage of time—a creed I had renounced in my misfortune, spoke enough and in sufficient candor to cede that you, too, had been acquainted with the night eclipse of human circumstance; until, away from that place, I could look at your kind eyes in the blazing noon of a more hopeful day and say: Dear friend, normal angel, going about your city errands, discouraged in many ways, doubting that you will be a luminary in our mortal world, dear friend, you are emblazoned in the pantheon, a private redemption, a fierce, immaculate light, a heroine.

THREE YEARS LATER

Basking in the simplest things, silky feet of the children, the way the morning light, let in, flings itself, anointing everything, rich sleep, no dreams, language for forgotten things, order and grace satisfying, music exultant, hope, shy at the door, not yet daring to come in, acrid taste of bitterness an amulet in my pocket, warding off cowardice, memory's assault defused, no longer lethal at first blast, the future tense, giving without exacting vengeance, less impatience, real hunger, fists unclenched, believable devotion making a return appearance: I, in my own name, assemble the shards into a clumsy pot, a vessel once exclusively for priests more suited now to daily transportation, taking me from here to there, useful confirmation that even when buried deep enough to resist all salvation, harder than elemental substance, not yielding to the most delicate solicitation, I can be found, fragment by fragment, uncovered by the tiny brushes of your kindness and attention, able after time to resurrect my voice, the world atoning for bereavement, delivering secret gifts, allowing me to make this declaration.

HERE I SIT

Here I sit, at the pivot of death and the resurgent current, composed of the places I have been and desire's memory in blood and skin, men, children. My body, loathed and beloved. My heart, afraid, willing to take everything in. My brain, made cynical by unsought experience, brilliant diagnostician.

It is the turning of the year, and I am still here, persevering, belligerent, consoled by darkness, a lover of midnight, engaged as always in the quest for tranquillity and sustaining light. Outside, the city stills. Inside me, an astonishing garden of lust and bravery flowers in an instant. Enormous music, exploding in every cell, makes me everyone I have loved, all of you, now, at the year's transformation, end of the century, charge of the millennium.

Come into my room. Comfort me, unknown women, take me in your myriad arms, mothers, daughters, sisters, others before and past this time. Take my words and let them live, wrench me from the particular into the sublime. Ill and well, we are entirely in this moment alive.

LOVE AS STRONG AS DEATH

Unquenched after all these years, a thirst for love that is not consumed, incarnate and transcendent, carnal and immaculate, innocent. Can I embody you, be a dwelling place for a spirit that partakes of all that lasts, encompassing mistakes, and appetites, and prodigal generosity, and terror and absolution, and whatever is most frightening about becoming human. You, carrying your pail ahead of me, spilling mercy and forgiveness daily, calling my name at the same moment I am conjuring you, a voice of unpolluted clarity, half a world away, beside, within me. You, my theological relief, my proof that even in the midst of unslaked cruelty at the end of a barbaric century, nothing less than a divinity could have tendered what you give me, and allowed that in my being on earth I give to you.

Incantation

FOR A GOOD DEATH

Grant the one who's lying in the bed an end to pain, ruthless, without shame.

Grant that as the body fails, dreams become a refuge for the bruised and weary heart.

Keep her company in the dark, and when the hour nears, make it easy to depart.

LEAVE-TAKING

Lullaby and good night, grow light
A new day arrives, close your eyes
Turn and return: you were born
The gift that was given is gone.

FOR WHOLENESS

If I must wake, let my soul regenerate and not mistake,
as I do now, a part for the whole: wholly beloved still
in your sight.

AGAINST THE FEAR OF DYING

I ask you, presence, immanent in all things
to let my fortitude transcend my fear
and bring innate, dispassionate love to bear
on my constricted soul, with healing wings.

UNREALISTIC CHANT FOR MY CHILDREN

No sorrow
no wretchedness
loss or despair:
joy and vitality
each day born fair.
No grieving
no hopelessness
death or delay:
ease and tranquillity
at close of day.

A Gathering of Women

A GATHERING OF WOMEN

THE SEEKER: When the bad news comes, how can you bear it?

THE INNOCENT: I tell myself: I'm strong enough; I can handle it. But at that moment I wanted to jump out the window.

THE ELDER: My mind swings into gear: What can I do to get moving? Where do I go from here?

THE CYNIC: I rage: How could God do this to me?

THE SEEKER: At least you believe in God.

THE MYSTIC: What place does this have in a larger story? That's what I want to know.

THE HEALER: I take a breath.

THE LOVER: I brace myself and say: You knew this was coming—no matter what it is. I always know I'm happy way beyond my just desserts.

THE PHILOSOPHER: My mind says: The moment is not the grand scheme; the moment simply is.

THE DREAMER: I tell myself: Don't complain; this is nothing; the bad thing hasn't happened yet.

THE SEEKER: What frightens me is further sorrow. You can't buy safety through suffering.

THE PRAGMATIST: But that makes me part of humanity. My losses connect me to the troubles of other people in a way I wasn't before. The death of my child defines who I am. It proves that I can face the worst tragedy and go on.

THE SAINT: My early grief was mixed with so much shock it doesn't even count as grief. It took six months before the terror and panic stopped, and the welling sadness began.

THE PRAGMATIST: Afterward, the protective bubble has burst. I don't live in fear of tragedy, but I know it's out there, a possibility.

THE ARTIST: When I was a child, I'd think: I'm learning to make a collection of the experiences of being alive. A big part of the collection is bad feelings. It was great to be getting more for my collection.

THE SEEKER: What have you learned that you would want other women to know?

THE ARTIST: Nobody I ever respected, ancient or modern, said that life is about happiness. It's not about being happy—or even about being sad. It's not about getting what you want. It seems to be an arbitrary journey over which you have very little control. Once you know that, there's something heroic about being a human being—just trying to get through it.

THE HEALER: I grow comforting to myself, like a mother to her daughters. When you imagine yourself as one of your daughters, you have to stop torturing yourself.

THE PHILOSOPHER: In her visions, St. Julian saw a God who was gentle, patient—and very maternal. "And you shall see for yourself that every kind of thing will be well," she said. There's nothing too small not to be made better.

THE SAINT: Happiness is something you search for from childhood, in its original form and in many sham forms. But grief is something you don't choose. So when it comes to you, it's real. You feel abandoned, not cared for, unconnected to any love. But if you believe in God, you know that in a world of good and evil, God comes down on the side of the good and is grieving along with you. I don't think God wills tragedy. Tragedy is part of the universe, and God is saying: I hate this.

THE MOTHER: No matter what befalls me, I feel commanded to choose life. You cannot give in to despair. You may hit bottom, but even then you have a choice. And to choose life means an obligation not merely to survive, but to live.

Sanctuary

LIBRARY

The words of another who's been there and knows, or someone quite other, a life unsuspected, or stories invented, tender and longing, or tales of praise, even heartache, wrongdoing. Centuries of wisdom or yesterday's news, trite verse that comforts or wormwood that soothes. The phrase that intuits that you, too, are part of the bitter adventure, sentences gripping until, at the end, you reluctantly part from someone who's translated her life into yours, and has dared to sacrifice silence in favor of words.

CEREMONY

Light a candle, bless the new moon, walk in white
gardens at the hour you used to, draw a filling breath
when the air is mild, retrieve early stories to offer a
rapt child, remember ancestors, mark the turning year,
celebrate festivals that once you could not bear, honor
ties of blood and affinity, return what you were lent,
hallow the ordinary meal that, shared with the same
friend in every season, becomes a sacrament.

WATER

Something about looking at water, the expanse of it, the way its skin can reflect a sheltering sky or repel like an old gray sheet, wrinkled from countless bodies, something about its depths and constancy, and the sound it makes at the edge, licking the old wood of the pier rhythmically, something about its auguring motion and turmoil and an intuition of the sea, something about its mirroring impermanence, and eternity.

True Words

WOLFE

Teacher, it took me more than twenty years to see myself as you could see me when we met, I in my youth and you flush with the plenitude of your deeds. How could we know that at your death each of us would find that you loved multitudes, one by one, or that you called your orphaned sisters and brothers every week before the Sabbath peace, or that years after you departed, we, the ones you left, would try to love with your gusto and irreverence because each night that you were home you called your oldest brother and spoke to him about your troubles, and eased his, before you said good night.

AUNT

The colors for spring are navy and red, and children never forget a beautifully set table, you told us as we sat around your kitchen, teasing you about such unassailable pronouncements. You were good and your ending bitter: All our love could not avert the harsh decree. And yet your love accompanies us, your nieces, who smile at your name and dream that we could tell you—now that it is too late—that yours turned out to be the constancy we need. We wanted to show you the new children; we wanted you to wear red and navy until you were very old, surrounded by descendants from two continents. We thought you would always wait for us in your kitchen, as you did when we were little, for the festival to begin, the table set with silver, and laughter rocking us into night.

UNCLE

One more Jewish child of history, you listened to the
rhythmic rage of Cossacks seeking entry in an early-
twentieth-century pogrom, your father far in Canada,
your mother terrified, you, nine years old, leaving
home by boat with all your fabled memories. A
greenie, damaged, proud of your equally fabled name,
you raised four children through the hard work of your
hands, and when you beat the odds to die at a respect-
able old age, we sat in your immaculate rooms and
thought of the way you painted and repainted your
own house, and that you never once were heard to
curse, and then the mailman came inside to say you
were a gentleman.

GRANDFATHER

The apple of your eye, I write these words more than thirty years after you left, having lit my childhood days. "He died like a dog," your youngest son still says, but lived like a prince of learning and a courtier of ill fortune. Today you would be older than the century that took you early, and in my dining room my daughter's grandfather looks at her with an adoring gaze and says, in his seventieth year, "Her whole life lies before her." Like many a conventional phrase, his words make my eyes smart with the same tears I could not cry for you when your head hurt and you spoke only Yiddish on a peculiar bed until you disappeared.

MATTIE

Your sister holds my daughter, your namesake, in her arms. Ninety-four years old, she utters in delight the name she spoke for almost a century: Mattie. Cold angel, your mother called you, brilliant and dispassionate, your silence a limpid refuge for my scorched intensity. Mattie, how astonished you would be to learn that every night I dream of seeing your face in the summer house you had for fifty years, welcoming me with food and tact, the ability to read all afternoon without our needing to exchange one word. When I told you that I missed you, you informed me I did not. Mattie, grandmother, I did, and miss you still.

RICHARD

In 1966 you were younger than I am now, when you bounded into class to make us think. Out of an ancient slumber we began to contemplate the headlines and the news you brought of Shakespeare, advertising's impact, art, Antigone, and the Jews. What happened to you and the young wife we met when we dared to visit you at home, a line drawing of a naked woman on your wall; we did not laugh. One spring day the following year, reading the paper as I tanned my legs, I came upon your name before these words: Arrested for stealing razor blades and nylons from a Dominion store. "Teachers and policemen are society's most important employees," you used to say, "and they are paid the least." For many years we wanted to take out an ad in *The Globe and Mail*, that newspaper you showed us how to read, pleading for news of you. Not long ago in a documentary on the First World War, I saw a photograph of a young soldier that evoked your face. You had a ginger mustache and a wiry body. Sixty-three this year, I calculate, you taught us to dissect an English sentence, our homely syllables transformed into a map of elegance.

DANIEL

Sick with love you silenced me, and I, relieved to let you go, find that, ten years past, your words continue to explain the world. Beauty, you said, what is it? A quarter-inch beneath our skins we are alike. Or how you stood beside me to illuminate the green of Manet's painting: Words poured from you, psalmist that you were. Exhausted after hours of staring, we repaired to a restaurant to contemplate again our perplexing love, a lethal brew of mishap and desire. Once I called you, saying that all my life, even if we never spoke again— and we have not—I would remember what I'd learned, unique, from you, to which you said: The rage I bear you is my cherished treasure. Old friend, still, in the silence, longer now than all the years we spoke, I hear your sleepy voice instructing me in what it means to live in this blunt world with the idea of perfect language.

Harvest

NAAMI

The symmetry of leaving earth with friends is not allotted in this ragged life. We debate: When you and I grow old, which one ought to go first, to spare the other pain. But that choice is not offered us. What we can choose, and do, is perishable, imperfect love, intimate with loss and bound to it. To let go. All things die and love dies, too, yet ours revived. Its healing made me fierce and adamant: Give us a natural parting in old age, completed lives, our children raised, indifferent to each other, like children forced to play together, our husbands tolerant, you mocking my distress at wrinkled flesh, me tender of your eccentricities. Neither to save nor be saved, not remarkable, Lord, transmute a passionate youth, grant two mortal friends an ordinary life.

LIZ

If I could change my fate for yours, I would not have the courage to endure what you have undergone. You say each person's pain is absolute and that the music keeps you steadfast through the nights and days. In our enlightenment and dismay, we yearn for one sustaining friend who will, with laughter and benevolence, cure us of the dark escorts that refuse to go away. May we be friends until a most benign and eloquent old age allows us to ease toward the end like a swimmer who, in very early morning, slips naked into a summer lake, before the mists have parted, before the others wake.

ROSE

There are worse things than to be loved for our yellow
hair, Rose. You give me clothes for my new daughter,
and your sage sentences about our quest for one mea-
sure of peace and loveliness accompany me through
many dark hours. I picture you in a long dress, making
tea in summer, your garden green at dusk. We talk
about our books and paintings, daughters of the fifties,
still astonished to be summoned by vocation.

FRIEND IN ANOTHER COUNTRY

Champagne of my life, your name is your fate, to
bestow upon us mortals, less adept, the gifts of food
and grace, a life of hard work interlaced with comfort,
the well-chosen chair, friends everywhere, a clarity of
purpose almost ruthless, through which we see ourselves, enhanced by your secular benediction: pleasure
on two continents, the book that never dies, what we
must immediately do or wear, unsated hunger for for-
eign skies coupled with the ability to live well in the
precise place we are.

BARBARA

God, I might have said, or providence, in your Texas parlance, brought me to your presence, guide I did not gauge to be sufficient. You lean against your chair and laugh as I unpack my grief, bleak surrender to an austere destiny. "Plants grow into light, and people, too, no matter how old or what travail," you state, not a determinist position but practical as the children's teacher you once were. I enter my fortieth year, middle, I hope, of a life that will prove wiser, more audacious, season of ripe revolt and fine accord. Defiant of the doomsayers, I record my jubilation.

HOUSE OF DREAMS

Razed to the ground, this was the house whose screened porch saw me dream of being translucent as an angel, through whom the light of summer poured endlessly, of love as recompense, of beauty. This was the dock on which a sixteen-year-old girl lay, tawny and lovelier than she knew, listening to the river, drifting from sun to shade, green fingers of shadow through which she swam into light, arms praising the sun and then plunging through darkness, like putting on sleeves of water. This was the night in which she slept on an iron bed under satin quilts, lulled by the crunch of gravel, crickets, and from far away the faint murmur of boats going out to sea. This was the moon under which her grandmother walked late at night, everyone sleeping, blood-orange slip of a moon and a skein of stars as ornaments, the universe continually expanding, life not an idle oar, a cake to be made, and the air briskly auguring winter. Comfort me with apples, she thought, alone, harvesting love.

An Old Tale

AN OLD TALE

The woman grieving by the road was given this consolation: Go to every house that has known no sorrow
and plead for flour. If from that flour you bake a cake
before night comes, the one you mourn will be returned.

She ran from house to house, but each refused
her. One door, then another, closed to her. The sky
whitened and grew dark, an empty bowl.

"Alas," the woman cried, "I am undone. Not one
would help me bring my lost one home."

Then she felt a hand upon her head. "My child,"
a voice said.

She saw the compassionate face and understood:
No house is immune from sorrow, and no woman from
a time of solitude.

Nessa Rapoport is the author of a novel, *Preparing for Sabbath*. Her short stories and essays have been published widely. With Ted Solotaroff, she edited the anthology *Writing Our Way Home*. She lives in New York with her husband and children.

Rochelle Rubinstein Kaplan is a Toronto painter and printmaker. Her work has been exhibited in Canada, the United States, and Europe. Her artist's books are in the collections of the Museum of Modern Art and the New York Public Library, among others.